# ST. LOUIS HILLS

RIVER DES PERES

JAMIESON

STREET

EICHELBERGER

School Site

JAM

AVENUE

PRATHER

PLAINVIEW AVE.

LANSDOWNE AVE.

WALSH ST.

DELOR ST.

ITASKA ST.

NEOSHO ST.

School Site

AVENUE

IVANHOE AVE.

WATSON

DONOVAN AVE.

AVENUE

AVE.

ROAD

RANCIS PARK.

MURDOCH

DEVONSHIRE

LANSDOWNE AVE.

SUTHERLAND AVE

BANCROFT AVE

CHILDRESS

AVE.

TAMM AVE.

NOTTINGHAM

PRAGUE AVE.

AVE.

ST.

ST.

ST.

VIENNA AVE.

IFTON AVENUE

WALSH ST.

DELOR ST.

ITASKA ST.

NEOSHO

LOCKE AVE

DEVONSHIRE AVE.

AVENUE

ST.

HAMPTON

CHIPPEWA

# ST. LOUIS HILLS

## BY ANN ZANABONI

REEDY PRESS
St. Louis, Missouri

Reedy Press, PO Box 5131, St. Louis, MO 63139, USA

Library of Congress Control Number: 2008935009

ISBN: 978-1-933370-31-6

Unless otherwise noted, images were obtained from the St. Louis Hills Neighborhood Association or from St. Louis Hills residents past and present.

Please visit our website at www.reedypress.com.

Printed in the United States of America
08 09 10 11 12 5 4 3 2 1

# CONTENTS

# ACKNOWLEDGMENTS

This book could not have been possible without the past efforts of the St. Louis Hills History Guild. The members who collected information over the years were unfailingly helpful and generous. Their documents and pictures have been donated to the Missouri History Museum. Thank you!

A special thank you to all the St. Louis Hills residents and former residents who contributed information to this book, including Ginny Nester, Richard Palank, Arthur Jeanette, Mary Lee Dooling, Mitch Hanneken, Colette and Martin Walsh, Joe Edwards, Bob and Marie Mudd, Rich Messmer, Andy, Ruth, and Celeste Kocot, and Liz Evola to name a few. NiNi Harris lent her invaluable knowledge and talent to this book. Thank you also to my family, Paul, Dominic, Joey, Tori, Mia, Hope, and Mary Zanaboni, for their support and patience as I wrote *St. Louis Hills*.

# FOREWORD

Urbanism uniting with suburbanism was what real estate developer Cyrus Crane Willmore envisioned in his conceptualization of a complete community designed to be almost a city unto itself. The far-sighted Willmore took a significant parcel of undeveloped land, and much like a sculptor, he and his team molded it into the carefully crafted St. Louis Hills. Willmore embarked on this Herculean endeavor in the bright days just before the darkness of the Depression descended on us. He wisely selected Francis Park as the heart of the Hills and enlisted the aid of some of the area's premier planners, builders, craftsmen, artisans, and real estate salesmen to turn his developmental strategy into reality.

When the brashness of the brassy 1920s became tarnished by the grimness and crises of the 1930s, a multitude of real estate developments, many considerably less flamboyant than the creation of St. Louis Hills, either were totally abandoned, truncated, or put on the proverbial back-burner. But Cyrus Crane Willmore's will and vision helped him see beyond the gloom. To the amazement of most observers, rather than retreat, he moved his plan forward, a tad less quickly as hoped, but the work advanced almost without missing a beat. With most building projects stalled or stopped in the St. Louis area, he had his choice of highly skilled workers in the construction trades—from architects to laborers—who were anxious to work. He ballyhooed the money to carry out his goals. Streets were created, sewers laid, his trademark pink sidewalks poured, trees planted, and buildings started going up—not Sears-Roebuck mail order nor frame houses, but solid masonry structures created in a wildly wide variety of architectural designs incorporating an incredible array of ornamentation. Willmore, a showman on a par with P. T. Barnum, created a sensation with the opening ceremonies for the first Hills home eight months after "the Crash." He put on an all-day show offering free refreshments, music, dancers, singers, most every civic leader, as well as our town's leading personality of the time, Ed Lowery, who was master of ceremonies at the Ambassador Theatre. Ed unlocked the door of the house, and the attending masses traipsed through the building that would be the seed from which St. Louis Hills grew.

By the time Prohibition passed, St. Louis Hills was prospering. Willmore and his staff, such as master salesman Frank Carbonetti, started it all by selling the sizzle, and now they were selling the steak. This neighborhood of tomorrow, like a magnet, was attracting home-buyers and businesses at a level comparable to that of the development of the West End and Central West End at the time of the 1904 World's Fair. Today, you will find over fifty streets in the well-forested St. Louis Hills neighborhood ranging from its longest, Hampton Avenue, which forms the Hills eastern border for some twenty blocks. Other somewhat harder to locate streets include a few that are just a block in length such as Crane Circle, Prather Avenue, Vienna Avenue, and Keith Place. Certain streets are continuations of those entering St. Louis Hills from the north or east such as Tamm, Finkman, and Holly Hills Avenues. Residents of the area are frequently asked why some of the streets bear names of places in England. That's due to a man named Everett Horton, English by birth, who owned considerable property just east of St. Louis Hills. When he sold a parcel of his land, he insisted he be allowed to name the streets for places in his former homeland. Hence we have Devonshire, Sutherland, Nottingham, and Lansdowne in St. Louis Hills as well as in Southhampton, now nicknamed SOHA, which is on the east side of Hampton Avenue.

The strength and success of St. Louis Hills started with the utopian prescience of Cyrus Crane Willmore and continues today through the efforts of those who live and have lived on the streets of this unique neighborhood. The residents are well supported with the work of the St. Louis Hills Neighborhood Association, the Hampton-Chippewa Business Association, the city of St. Louis, the Metropolitan St. Louis Police Department, conscientious businesses, and the churches and parochial schools.

Architecture influences us all. We respond to the forms and spaces we encounter, and in no small way this is true in St. Louis Hills where the building arts have provided a catalyst in which those experiencing them can grow and prosper. We give a special tip of the Rabbitt hat to Cyrus Crane Willmore, whose dream live on.

Ron (Johnny Rabbitt) Elz

# INTRODUCTION

St. Louis Hills is a neighborhood tucked into the southwest corner of the city. It is a beautiful blend of urban conveniences and suburban style—a neighborhood rich in history, culture, community spirit, and family traditions.

The earliest records for the land that would become St. Louis Hills indicate that the property was a designated land grant in 1768 from Pierre Laclede to Ann Camp and her son-in-law Antoine Reilhe. It was later sold to George C. Clark for $11,700. Clark gave the property to his two sons. The land was divided equally. Its division

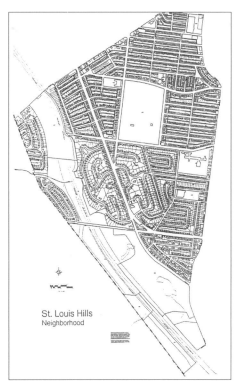

St. Louis Hills
Neighborhood

The St. Louis Hills Neighborhood.

was marked by a lane called Clark Road, which later became Eichelberger Street. These tracts of land were barren hunting land rumored to be popular with "moonshiners." There was reportedly a lake south of Clark Road.

In 1884, David R. Francis—who served as mayor of St. Louis, governor of Missouri, secretary of the Interior under President Grover Cleveland, ambassador to Russia during the Russian Revolution, and president of the 1904 World's Fair—bought the land. Francis considered this tract of land for the World's Fair, but because it was not accessible to public transportation, the plan never materialized.

David R. Francis (right) poses with Grover Cleveland and Theodore Roosevelt.

David R. Francis donated land for the creation of Francis Park, shown below.

David R. Francis was a visionary. He had been negotiating for several months with the commissioner of Parks and Recreation, Nelson Cunliff. They knew that the southwest corner of the city was ripe for development. Cunliff was eager to build a park in the area before land got too expensive. On Christmas Eve of 1916, St. Louisans streamed downtown to 12th Street to see the municipal tree lighting and to see Santa Claus (portrayed by a man name Otto Karbe) deliver the deed granting part of "Francis Farm" to the city. The *St. Louis Republic* called his generous gift "an immortal thing." The restrictions were few, but clear. The property was to be used for park and recreational purposes only, and it would be maintained by the city. If anyone ever tried to use the land for other purposes, it would revert back to Francis or his heirs. This sixty-acre tract, the crown jewel of the area, was to forever be known as Francis Park. The remainder of the farm was later sold as land to be developed.

World War I delayed any serious park improvements for several years, but in November 1923, Cunliff, who had since been made St. Louis's director of Public Welfare, announced a novel plan. Under his direction, first-time offenders from the City Workhouse were encamped on the grounds of Francis Park. They were enlisted to do the landscaping, clean-up, and other work that would transfer a chunk of farmland into a first-class city park. Fourteen men arrived at the park on November 6. "They are men who have made but one bad step, have offended but once, and who want to live down that one bad mistake. They will be workmen serving out their time as honest labor for the city," said Cunliff. With this unique, but effective approach, the director of Public Welfare set Francis Park on its way.

In 1929, Cyrus Crane Willmore, a prominent St. Louis real estate developer, envisioned Francis Park as the center of a "dream" neighborhood. He foresaw a prominent community with tree-lined streets surrounding this lovely enclave. Willmore bought the remaining Francis property and began the building of the original St. Louis Hills.

Cyrus Crane Willmore (center) poses with Cardinal J. J. Glennon and Bishop Donnelly.

Cyrus Willmore's Development Office, 1928.

Along with Willmore's property was a small tract of land called the Freber Farm. In the early 1900s, the Frebers, a German-American family, ran and lived on their truck farm that produced tomatoes, string beans, iceberg lettuce, onions, and horseradish and trucked them to the Fourth Street market. The farm was profitable for more than twenty-five years. The large farmhouse sitting in the front of the property served as the main family home. Behind it was a small, three-room farmhouse for Freber's daughter and son-in-law.

The homes had neither electricity nor running water, and the farm was irrigated by a nearby stream that was later condemned for irrigation because it one day reportedly "bubbled up black and smelly," according to an article in the *St. Louis Globe-Democrat.* For a while the family and workers carted water to the farm, but when Cyrus Willmore wanted to buy the land to add to St. Louis Hills, the Frebers decided the time was right to sell. This integral piece of land became the corner of Jamieson and Chippewa Avenues, an important part of the neighborhood.

After acquiring all of the property, Willmore immediately began survey work for the new streets around Francis Park. Surveyor

Frederick Pitzman was engaged to make a layout for the St. Louis Hills subdivision. Willmore grew St. Louis Hills out from the park, situating churches opposite each of the park's four corners, building impressive single-family homes and apartment buildings, and laying the neighborhood's famous pink sidewalks as a touch of class. To make the site more accessible to the city, he put $46,000 on the table to subsidize a bus line from St. Louis Hills to an existing streetcar line.

St. Louis Hills' reputation as a premiere neighborhood was no accident. Willmore carefully, but relentlessly marketed his project to St. Louisans seeking refuge from the noise, smells, and uncertainties of urban life, advertising "country living in the city." In the first issue of the Cyrus Crane Willmore Organization's first official magazine, *News of St. Louis Hills,* he promised "prices are right, surroundings are beautiful, children are happy, neighbors are congenial and everyone is concerned about matters which constitute right living." Willmore worked hard to maintain that St. Louis Hills was the manifestation of the American ideals of hard work, home ownership, and the nuclear family.

While home construction in St. Louis Hills proceeded somewhat slowly during the Depression, Willmore continued to commit himself to the neighborhood. Toward the end of World War II, Willmore filed four plats known as St. Louis Hills Estates. These plats were bordered by Eichelberger Street on the north, Gravois Avenue on the south, Hampton Avenue on the east, and the River Des Peres on the west. His entire development became collectively known as St. Louis Hills, encompassing the sprawling 750 acres that was originally farmland.

As the neighborhood grew, so did the need for schools in the area. In 1952, two schools, identical in plan, opened in St. Louis Hills. These school were built to replace the portable school buildings that had been in place for a number of years. Nottingham School at 4915

right: Greater St. Louis Hills Home Owners Association Constitution and Bylaws.

following spread: An aerial view of St. Louis Hills, October 9, 1936: (1) Francis Park; (2) Public Schools Portables; (3) St. Gabriel; (4) Hampton Avenue; (5) Adolphus Busch School; (6) Cyrus Crane Willmore Organization, Inc. office; (7) St. Louis Hills No. 2; (8) St. Louis City Limits; (9) River Des Peres; (10) Junction of Watson and Highway 66; (11) Gravois Road; (12) Mississippi River.

GREATER ST. LOUIS HILLS
HOME OWNERS ASSOCIATION

CONSTITUTION and BY-LAWS

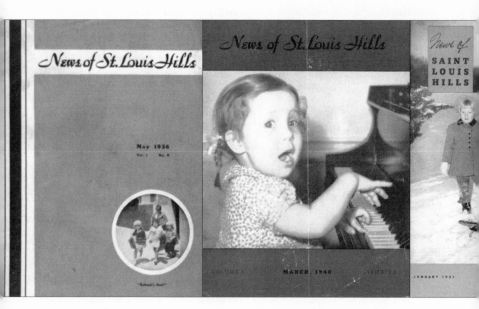

May 1936                                    March 1940

Donovan Avenue and the Adolphus Busch School at 5910 Clifton Avenue, which was named after the famous brewer, were both designed by architect F. Ray Leimuehler.

Bishop Louis DuBourg High School was originally located in several buildings at Jefferson Barracks beginning about 1950. It remained there until 1954, when the present building at 5850 Eichelberger Street was completed from plans by architects Murphy and Mackey. At the time of its erection, DuBourg High School was said to be the largest structure to be built in the Archdiocese of St. Louis since the completion of the New Cathedral in 1914. The school's seventeen-acre site had been purchased earlier by the late Cardinal John J. Glennon. The completed school building was dedicated by Archbishop Joseph Ritter on September 12, 1954. At that time it had a capacity of 1,600 students, and in 1956 it was enlarged by a twenty-room annex at its western end, increasing the capacity to 2,200.

August 1951                                          April 1952

A NEIGHBORHOOD OF BEAUTIFUL HOMES, SCHOOLS AND CHURCHES

AR—Vol. 17, No. 9          SOUTH ST. LOUIS, MO., WEDNESDAY, MAY 11, 1977

Class Thomas Hartmann,
d Mrs. Al Hartmann, of
eet, has been awarded the
scholarship for graduate
anities.
ior at the United States

The true stability of St. Louis Hills was readily apparent. The neighborhood retained its charm, and the houses quickly appreciated in value. Longtime residents, their children, and their children's children, continued to live in and take care of the neighborhood. Built on the foundations of family, tradition, and community, St. Louis Hills consistently remained a strong pocket of middle- to upper-class standing in the city of St. Louis. Its rich history, coupled with the strong community spirit, provided an ideal neighborhood to raise a family.

The Compton Heights Concert Band of Saint Louis

Kaid Friedel, Director

performing at

Francis Park

Donovan and Eichelberger

Tuesday, August 26th
7:30pm

Sponsored by: The Greater Saint Louis Hills Homeowners' Association; The Music Performance Trust Funds, Local 2-197 American Federation of Musicians and The Missouri Arts Council.

Compton Heights Band

left: Communication has always been a key to the neighborhood's success. *St. Louis Hills News* shared information with residents during the 1970s.

top and right: Summer concerts in Francis Park are an enduring neighborhood tradition.

top: Bishop DuBourg High School.

bottom: Adolphus Busch School.

top: A neighborhood soccer team poses for a picture after a game at Nottingham School. circa 1977.

bottom: Nottingham School's cornerstone ceremony.

Brides are common sight during the summer months around St. Louis Hills. Here, former *Post-Dispatch* outdoors columnist James A. Kearns, Jr., poses outside his home at 6236 Walsh Street with his daughter, Marie Claire, on her wedding day, June 1, 1963.

# Chapter 1
# HOME SWEET HOME

O n a sunny Sunday in July 1930, twelve thousand people descended on the first model home in St. Louis Hills at 6226 Itaska Street. The crowds came to see the much-anticipated "ideal" home built by the Cyrus Crane Willmore Organization. They were not disappointed! The event was staged after months of preparation by Willmore. The ceremony was lively and the advertisements enticed visitors with "cold ice water." The entire block opposite the model home, built by contractor Hugh J. Karr, was reserved as an automobile parking lot for the convenience of the scores who attended the opening ceremony.

A peppy atmosphere contributed to the excitement of the opening ceremony. The first-built house was considered a show piece. According to *City Beautiful,* a monthly magazine reflecting the growth and development of St. Louis, "The speeches were short, snappy and stimulating . . . and there was plenty of ice water and fresh air as the President of the Board of Alderman stressed several times." True to fashion, Willmore kept the ceremony brief, and the doors to the model home were unlocked with a flourish promptly at 1:30 p.m. This was the beginning of the neighborhood.

top: The first model home in the neighborhood was at 6226 Itaska Street.

bottom: The first model home was opened to a celebratory crowd in July 1930.

Cyrus Willmore celebrates the first model home with some friends. From left to right: John W. Higgenbor-ham, vice president and general sales manager; Frank Carbonetti, salesman; four-year-old Sally Laux; Willmore; unknown; Judge Walter J. Neun, president of the Board of Aldermen; Maurice J. Cassidy, sec-retary of the Building Trade Council.

An interior of an early model home.

# If You Build It...

C harles Micotto was instrumental in developing St Louis Hills. He paved the streets, laid the sewers, and created the side-walks all before the houses were built. According to Micotto's son and successor, Vincent Micotto, it took three years to lay the streets and sewers in St. Louis Hills. Eight hundred feet of sewer was reportedly laid each day. Micotto Construction used cast iron for the sewers, which was considered the newest and most effective material. The one draw back of cast iron is its inability to contract with heat and expand with cold. This is the reason for an occasional broken pipe in the neighborhood. It was certainly a better choice than the alternative in the early 1900s: lead.

# The Vedder Building

top: The apartment building at the corner of Nottingham and Clifton Avenues, known as the Vedder Building, is the perfect example of modern influence, Art Deco significance, and Gothic architecture. Widely heralded as a building of historic significance, this apartment building was completed in 1938. It attracted many visitors and became a highly sought-after residence. Mrs. Vedder, her daughter, and son-in-law occupied the two large seven-room penthouse apartments when it was built. The building also has four five-room apartments with janitor quarters, garage, and rathskeller in the basement. The luminous electric fountain in the front courtyard was deemed "simply beautiful" by News of St. Louis Hills, the neighborhood news magazine.

right: Adolf J. Vedder.

The Micotto family continued to work with Cyrus Willmore as houses were being built. Their company poured most of the foundations for the original homes. The Micottos were generous contributors to St. Gabriel the Archangel Church and School and did most of the concrete work at no cost to the parish. As the Depression neared, Willmore was strapped for money and offered to pay Charles Micotto with a brand new house. Micotto took him up on the offer and moved his family into the display home on Itaska in 1931. Vincent Micotto also loved the neighborhood, and he and his wife purchased a house at 6441 Murdoch in 1934 and lived there for sixty-seven years.

Willmore's sales force was numerous, but George Overmeyer was instrumental in the sales of the lots in the neighborhood. The sought-after properties were selling for about sixty dollars a foot or more, with each lot measuring approximately thirty-five feet. Willmore was a well-connected businessman, and many important people were close to him. Harry S Truman was present for the dedication of the first home built at 6226 Itaska Street.

The homes in the neighborhood featured modern amenities for the era. The time was right for the use of new building materials. Cast concrete, aluminum, and glass block were coming into vogue. Many homes in St. Louis Hills were built as expressions of the Art Deco movement, which surged in popularity in the 1930s. One of the most unusual, yet historically significant homes in St. Louis Hills was built just west of Francis Park at 6520 Itaska Street. This eight-sided house became well-known in the architectural community. The fact that each side differed in length and the truly ingenious structure, combined with the lovely façade, made this house an architectural gem.

top: **6201 Itaska Street.**

bottom: **6520 Itaska Street.**

# Houses in the Hills

Along with the beautiful Art Deco–style homes; there are many Tudor, Colonial, and stately two-story homes through-out the St. Louis Hills community. A New Orleans–style home with a second-floor balcony is also featured in the neighbor-hood. Still today, people are drawn to the architecture. No two houses in the neighborhood are exactly alike, adding to the unique spirit of the community. Willmore would give a final inspection to each and every house; moving a window or recreating an entryway to make the houses original. The houses, duplexes, and apartment buildings were built in the 1930s and 1940s. Hardwood floors, stained glass (often with a southwestern motif), elegant stone work, glass block trim, slate or tile roofs, casement and circular windows, and zigzag brick patterns characterize these structures.

The homes and apartments surrounding Francis Park typify much of the neighborhood. On Nottingham Avenue, which runs along the north side of Francis Park, it is easy to find examples of port-hole windows, zigzag brick, and lovely glass block. East and west of the park, stately two-story homes line Tamm and Donovan Av-enues. These single-family homes were advertised at a price of about $10,000 in 1934.

An Art Deco apartment complex at 5800 Devonshire.

The beautiful Tudor-style home at 6556 Delor Street.

top: The current house at 6381 Murdoch Avenue was constructed after the original home was demolished after a gas explosion.

right: Ashpits once lined the alleys of St. Louis Hills. Only a handful remain.

following spread: 6337 Nottingham was moved to make way for St. Gabriel the Archangel Church. Courtesy Arteaga Photos.

In the early 1930s, the two-family apartment building at 6337 Nottingham was moved to accommodate the building of St. Gabriel Church. The old-timers in the neighborhood clearly remember the event. As students, they stood outside St. Gabriel School at recess time and watched the moving process. The apartment building was loaded onto a moving truck and moved a "couple hundred feet." This enabled St. Gabriel Church and a driveway to be built. The building still stands just west of the driveway. It is said to have sustained no damage, just the distinction of being the "building that was moved." It was moved by EF David House Moving Company.

The beautiful house at 4701 Prague Avenue has a rich history as well as a lovely, traditional English style. The house was supposedly built by well-known St. Louis gangster Buster Wortman's right-hand man, Dutch Dowling. He built the house with bullet-proof windows. The house has no working fireplaces, which was novel in the 1930s. Dowling was reportedly fearful that a rival gangster would drop a bomb down a chimney. The lovely structure defies the turbulent history of the house, but it was one of the first Tudor-style houses built in the neighborhood.

On a cold Wednesday night in January 1963, the house at 6381 Murdoch Avenue was demolished by a gas explosion. The explosion killed Mrs. Kathryn Vander Pluym, sixty-six, and her invalid son Edward H. Vander Pluym, Jr., thirty-two. Mr. Edward H. Vander Pluym, Sr., sixty-seven, husband and father of the victims, was pulled—miraculously uninjured—from the rubble by neighbors. Gas service was shut off to the entire area after the explosion ruptured a main near the home. The subzero temperatures and ice made the resulting fire difficult to fight. A torn and tattered drape, apparently blown from the house, hung in a nearby tree. Firefighters battled the erupting fires through the night with ice-crusted coats and equipment. Neighbors turned on porch lights to assist the operations. St. Gabriel the Archangel Church made its facilities available to the workers.

4811-16-5

# The Life House

The "Life House" was another of Cyrus Crane Willmore's promotions. *LIFE* magazine sponsored a nation-wide home building program to build a "practical, visible demonstration of the latest and best in Modern American Homes." According to the *News of St. Louis Hills*, the house was built to be "a well blended combination of simplicity, convenience and good tastes—the three 'musts' in modern streamlined American living." The "Life House" was built at 6206 Devonshire Avenue. The special features included aluminum windows, both double hung and casement, a glass block window, fixtures exhibited at the New York World's Fair, "adequate wiring," and weatherproof outdoor sockets. In addition, the home was primarily run on natural gas, a true convenience of the time. Cooking, house heating, water heating, and refrigeration were newly run on natural gas, making this house updated and futuristic. Life House was a much-anticipated version of the family home. It was seen by thousands and advertised as the must-have modern home.

The McCall's "House of the Week" at 6359 Murdoch was a favorite of Cyrus Willmore.

The New Orleans–style home at 6359 Murdoch was a model home for the neighborhood. Its lovely two-story structure is dominated by a top-floor balcony. The brick, doors, and windows were painted white, which was unusual for the early 1930s. Cyrus Willmore was proud of this house; he attended the grand opening and first open house, showing people through the rooms himself.

top: The two-family home at 6337 Nottingham that was moved to accommodate the building of St. Gabriel Church.

bottom: The home at 4924 Tamm Avenue originally sold for about $40,000 in the early 1930s.

top: This home at 4701 Prague Avenue has a rich history and beautiful old-world charm.

# The Estates

The clearest division in architectural style can be seen by dividing the areas north and south of Eichelberger Street, which basically divides the area into St. Louis Hills and St. Louis Hills Estates. In St. Louis Hills Estates, there are primarily brick ranch homes that were built after World War II. These homes, also developed by the Cyrus Crane Willmore Organization, range from compact two-bedroom homes to elegant sprawling homes with large manicured yards. Large picture windows were a significant part of the architecture of these 1940s and 1950s homes. Many residents claim the windows were for showing off new furniture, a luxury after the war. In 1948, a three-bedroom ranch home was advertised for $40,000.

There were many renowned residents of the Estates, including the St. Louis Cardinals' baseball players Red Schoendeist, Joe Garagiola, and Stan Musial. Ron Northey, another St. Louis Cardinals Player, lived on Tamm Avenue in the original section of St. Louis Hills. Radio personality Ron Elz, also known as Johnny Rabbitt, resides in the Estates. Bob Burnes, the former *Globe-Democrat* sports columnist, was also a well-known resident of the Estates. Although he owned the house on Rhodes Avenue much later, his home had an interesting history. The houses in this particular block of Rhodes, between Childress and Clifton Avenues, were unique because they were built during World War II, an unusual occurrence as supplies and money were difficult to acquire. These houses were built for war workers.

A map showing a portion of the plots in the Estates.

Many of the ranch homes in the Estates have been updated and renovated. This particular home added a second story to the original structure.

Anthony Giordano, the reported head of the St. Louis Italian Mafia, was a resident of the Estates in the 1960s. He was well-known in St. Louis Hills and the Estates, although to many people in St. Louis, he went unobserved, living in a modest home and seeming to live a quiet life. Giordano was reportedly closely tied to the Jimmy Michaels family, head of the large and successful Syrian gang in St. Louis for many years. They worked closely together, and Jimmy Michaels was also a part of the St. Louis Hills neighborhood. He opened his restaurant in Hampton Village, where Target now stands. It was called Michael's Bar and Grill. In the 1970s, when Michaels came under attack by rivals sanctioned by mob leaders in Chicago, Gior-

dano was said to be able to guarantee Michaels' safety. However, when Giordano died at his home in the Estates in 1980, Michaels' safety net was gone and Michaels was killed within three weeks. It was rumored that St. Raphael's Catholic Church refused to bury Giordano due to his mob connections and sparse attendance at Mass.

*   *   *

St. Louis Hills is a community rich in history and detail. From small bungalows to large homes with expansive lawns, one idea remains consistent; this is a community proud of its tradition and committed to its neighborhood.

Many celebrated business and sports leaders have lived in stately homes in the Estates.

A lovely landscaped home in the Estates.

This home is a typical ranch-style house built with large front windows, a trend that was particularly popular after World War II.

Hampton Village, 2008.

# Chapter 2

# TAKING CARE OF BUSINESS

## Commerce and Places Remembered

In the early 1930s, few families had cars, so the "perfect" neighborhood provided everything within easy walking distance of home. Most housewives had their milk and butter delivered, the "egg man" came once a week, and baked goods were bought daily at neighborhood bakeries or delivered by Freund Bakery, a popular neighborhood establishment. Produce stands popped up regularly, as there was no such thing as one-stop-shopping until Hampton Village was built in the 1940s. Hampton Village, the main shopping des-

tination for the neighborhood, was built to serve the people of St. Louis Hills, making life in the neighborhood easier because of easy access to so many retailers in the city's first-ever, all-encompassing shopping mall.

Bettendorfs under construction.

# Hampton Village

H ampton Village included most of the intersection at Hampton and Chippewa, except the northwest corner. During the holidays, lines of cars waited to get into the parking lot. Theodore Vollmer Contracting was the general building contractor that developed and built Hampton Village. According to longtime residents, when Hampton Village was being built the contractor allowed children over age nine to roam the construction site picking up empty Pevely and Sealtest pint bottles. He would give the children two cents per bottle, making him a popular, well-known figure with the local kids.

Hampton Village was similar to the setup that still remains today. A grocery store was the first building at the site near the southeast corner of Hampton and Chippewa, which was, until that time, an open-air market called St. Louis Hills Market. The store, which was originally called Bettendorfs and later became Bettendorf-Rapp, faced Hampton, but it was close to Chippewa. Bettendorfs was the first large grocery store in St. Louis, and the people of the neighborhood loved it because it provided so much selection in one store. At the time, it was unique to have meat counters, a bakery, and countless grocery items in one store. Bettendorfs provided three different meat counters, each with a different grade of meat, an in-house bakery, a lunch counter, a restaurant, several cashiers, and a much larger selection of fruit and vegetables. Women came to rely on the convenience of this supermarket, making their daily lives easier, and children were regularly "sent up" to Bettendorfs to pick up groceries for their mothers. A new era in shopping had begun.

The strip mall behind the grocery store was built a few years later. J.C. Penney's was the anchor on the south end, and Walgreens, which included two floors and a post office, was the anchor on the north end. A few of the other stores that made an impact on the neighborhood included Garlands, a very popular women's clothing store; Libson, another women's clothing store; Kresges dime store; Anatel's Dress Shop; Arenson's men's clothing store; Keifer Jewelers; Etienne Coiffures; Warner-Noll Bake Shop; Penrose Shoe Co.; and many doctor and dentist offices. Weiler's Men's Wear, a later addition to Hampton Village, advertised Van Heusen

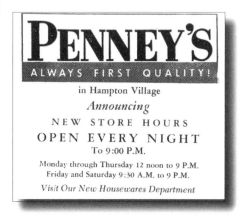

dress shirts for $2.95 in 1949. Krause Key, originally a tall, rough-looking structure standing just south of Bettendorf-Rapp, was the neighborhood's lock and key retailer. A side street off of Sulphur allowed access to Hampton Village, but the street was eventually closed as the strip mall kept expanding. As a promotional gimmick, Betten-

| Krause Key stands on the former site of Wilgen's Filling Station.

dorf-Rapp was called Schnuckendorf's when the chain was sold to Schnucks, who operated it until it was razed. Schnucks touted modern conveniences, large selections, and their "Schnucks Station" restaurant, which was a popular lunch destination with a railroad station motif. Children in the neighborhood loved to dine and have birthday meals at the Station Restaurant. They would get a small conductor hat and a train-themed placemat.

At the southwest corner of Hampton and Chippewa, the buildings were originally built in the same Williamsburg style as the buildings on the east side of Hampton. This structure was eventually demolished, and a more generic-looking building was erected. This eventually became Arlan's, a popular discount store. It sold many inexpensive items, including clothing and household goods. Arlan's was a well-liked neighborhood store, and St. Louis Hills residents were sorry to see it go. Next to Arlan's, near Chippewa, a well-known figure was always at his stand, rain or shine. Known as Sam the Watermelon Man, he sold whole watermelons to many families in the neighborhood. On the same lot, Michael's Bar, formerly known as Caswell's, was owned by the Michaels family and stood at this location for many years. It was rumored to have off-track betting in the basement, but no one could ever prove any wrongdoing. Some of the other retailers have included Bill Hartmann's Fine Ice Creams, which would deliver dairy products right to your door; Sweetins Flooring; Harmony Music; and a free-standing photo developing shop.

At the northeast corner of Hampton and Chippewa, also part of Hampton Village during the early years of the neighborhood, was another strip mall that consisted of small shops. Johnnie Brocks was a family run card store. It was rumored that Johnnie never turned on the lights in the store, trying to keep the electric bills low. Johnnie Brocks eventually changed hands and moved across Chippewa to Hampton Village. Catholic Supply became a popular shopping destination in the mid-1950s, relocating to its current location at the corner of Chippewa and Jamieson in the mid-1990s. The popular Stein Brother's Bowling Alley stood at the northwest corner of Chippewa and Hampton. Many neighborhood bowling leagues were formed over the years, with afternoon leagues being very popular with the housewives in St. Louis Hills.

Bettendorf-Rapp

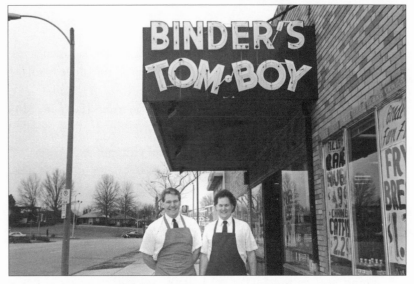

Brothers Jim (left) and Joe (right) LeGrand have owned LeGrands since 1987.

# Family Run Grocery Stores

U ntil Bettendorfs came to the neighborhood, small, family run grocery stores were the norm. The stock was limited and shopping was a daily event. Binders Tom-Boy Market, located at 4414 Donovan Avenue, was a family run market established in 1937 that served the neighborhood well. It was large compared to many markets, but it lacked the extensive choices available at the new larger grocery store. Binders originally shared the building on Donovan with a dry cleaners and a bakery. As Binders kept expanding, they took over the bakery and finally the dry cleaners, using the entire building for the market. Binders cut out a niche in the neighborhood and remained popular for many years, with their slogan, "Rain or Shine—We Deliver on Time," being well known around St. Louis Hills as many residents counted on Binders to deliver their groceries. Binders changed hands in 1987 to brothers and neighborhood residents Joe and Jim LeGrand. The market became LeGrands, but many longtime residents still refer to it as Binders. The small-market mentality was all but dead in St. Louis Hills, but the LeGrand brothers came up with the idea of ready-made food to serve at neighborhood functions. They specialized in neighborhood events like First Communion parties, graduation get-togethers, and block parties, touting full-service catering and mouth-watering made-to-order sandwiches. The market added a table and chair section for customers to enjoy their sandwiches in the store. The eat-in section was created between the bottles of wine and the deli counter, but it lent itself to the homey, old-time atmosphere for which LeGrands is widely known. The traditions at LeGrands kept customers coming back time and time again. The LeGrand brothers made sure each customer was greeted with a smile and the kids were always offered a smoky—a small, hot dog-type treat that's extremely popular at LeGrands (or Binders, if you were born before 1980).

above: **Binders Market in the early years.**

right: **An inside view of Binders in the early 1930s.**

Another well-remembered small grocery store, called Reliable, was located in a storefront on Hampton near Neosho, currently the site of Elite Beauty Salon. It was said to have canned goods stacked floor to ceiling, with a small amount of produce and dairy products. It served the neighborhood well until Bettendorfs made the store obsolete. The most memorable aspect of Reliable was its "reacher." Many former customers remember that they were discouraged from picking out their own canned goods. A long device on a pole that could reach up and grab a can was used to pluck items from near the ceiling.

It's "Flavor Plus"

## TOM BOY COFFEE

Sold Exclusively in Over 200 Tom Boy Stores

Originally, the Lansdowne Medical Building, at the corner of Chippewa and Lansdowne, was an A&P store that later became an IGA. The store burned in a spectacular fire around 1949. Years later, the current office building was built on that site. There was a Kroger store on the west side of Watson Road just north of Chippewa and a National supermarket a bit north of Chippewa on Watson. National later moved to where Schnucks' Hampton Village store is located today.

# Business in the Hills

Heading south on Hampton, many storefronts have come and gone. Some of the well-remembered included Winklemann Pharmacy at 5101 Hampton Avenue; Wilgen's Filling Station (which is now Krause Key), the neighborhood service station that stood at Hampton and Devonshire; and Schray's Florist, a convenient neighborhood spot to pick up fresh flowers, at the southwest corner of Hampton and Devonshire. Henry Hudson's pharmacy at 4924 Hampton at Neosho Avenue was another pharmacy that served the neighborhood, but it also advertised a soda fountain that attracted the younger crowds. Many youngsters sat at the counter, and for about a dime received soda fountain treats. Another pharmacy important to the neighborhood was Lindenwood Drug at Jamieson and Lansdowne. It remains a family run pharmacy with ideal customer service and personal commitment to the residents of St. Louis Hills.

In the early 1930s, several shops were thriving. Koch Brother's Floral Shop, a few blocks east of St. Louis Hills at 5210 Chippewa west of Brannon Avenue, sold flowers for every occasion. Lammerts Furniture was a longtime business at the corner of Chippewa and Jamieson, where Blockbuster now stands. It sold furniture to many families in the neighborhood. The Hoffmeister Colonial Mortuary was built in 1938 and was one of the first major businesses in the area. In order to build the current Hoffmeister Mortuary, a few of

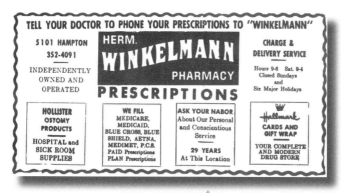

TELL YOUR DOCTOR TO PHONE YOUR PRESCRIPTIONS TO "WINKELMANN"

5101 HAMPTON
352-4091

INDEPENDENTLY
OWNED AND
OPERATED

HERM.
**WINKELMANN**
PHARMACY

**PRESCRIPTIONS**

CHARGE &
DELIVERY SERVICE

Hours 9-6   Sat. 9-4
Closed Sundays
and
Six Major Holidays

| HOLLISTER OSTOMY PRODUCTS<br>HOSPITAL and SICK ROOM SUPPLIES | WE FILL MEDICARE, MEDICAID, BLUE CROSS, BLUE SHIELD, AETNA, MEDIMET, P.C.S.<br>PAID Prescriptions PLAN Prescriptions | ASK YOUR NABOR About Our Personal and Conscientious Service<br>29 YEARS At This Location | Hallmark<br>CARDS AND GIFT WRAP<br>YOUR COMPLETE AND MODERN DRUG STORE |

Lindenwood Drug.

the neighborhood houses had to be demolished, which was an important, news-making story in the neighborhood. Hoffmeister remains on Chippewa at the corner of Childress Avenue. The Colonial style is still considered to be an architectural gem. Seligas was a popular delicatessen, which also sold a small amount of groceries. Interestingly, the proprietor was also St. Louis Hills' well-loved postman, Mr. Seliga. Being an ocean voyager, he also had his hand in booking passage for customers on ocean liners. Gilder's 66 was an automobile service station that advertised a handsome, smiling gentleman who could fill your gas tank or service your flat tire.

Many more businesses continue their service to the neighborhood today, including Leshers Florist, Clarice's Bridal Shop, Olympic Sporting Goods, St. Louis Hills Automotive, Nottingham Service Station, Slyman Brothers Appliances, and Nottingham Photography.

The St. Louis Hills Retirement Center, now called Provision Living in St. Louis Hills, at 6543 Chippewa, was originally built as the Congress Inn Hotel. It was very successful and lasted about ten years, until the new highways diverted traffic off of Chippewa. The retirement center was renovated many times and became a 108-unit assisted living community.

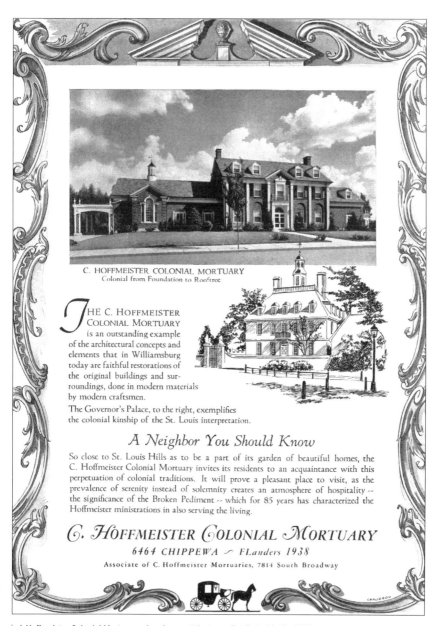

C. HOFFMEISTER COLONIAL MORTUARY
Colonial from Foundation to Rooftree

THE C. HOFFMEISTER COLONIAL MORTUARY is an outstanding example of the architectural concepts and elements that in Williamsburg today are faithful restorations of the original buildings and surroundings, done in modern materials by modern craftsmen.

The Governor's Palace, to the right, exemplifies the colonial kinship of the St. Louis interpretation.

## A Neighbor You Should Know

So close to St. Louis Hills as to be a part of its garden of beautiful homes, the C. Hoffmeister Colonial Mortuary invites its residents to an acquaintance with this perpetuation of colonial traditions. It will prove a pleasant place to visit, as the prevalence of serenity instead of solemnity creates an atmosphere of hospitality -- the significance of the Broken Pediment -- which for 85 years has characterized the Hoffmeister ministrations in also serving the living.

## C. HOFFMEISTER COLONIAL MORTUARY

### 6464 CHIPPEWA ✧ FLanders 1938

Associate of C. Hoffmeister Mortuaries, 7814 South Broadway

A Hoffmeister Colonial Mortuary advertisement that was distributed in the 1940s.

The Congress Inn, a well-known hotel, banquet facility, and meeting center, was opened in the 1950s and lasted about ten years.

# Restaurants

## Cafeteria-Style Delights

**M**any restaurants have served the neighborhood. Garavelli's Restaurant at the corner of Lansdowne and Chippewa became famous for its comfort-food cuisine in a cafeteria setting. The building that houses Garavelli's opened in 1941 as Joe Mittino's Shangri-La Supper Club and Seven Seas Lounge. Charlie Mittino opened a supper club at the site of Pietro's on Watson Road. Shangri-La offered a children's menu, receptions, and nightly dancing; the basement reportedly had aquariums built into the basement

Shangri-La was a particularly popular restaurant in the neighborhood in the early 1950s.

*Shangri-La*

"THE EPICURE'S PARADISE"
**FAMOUS CENTURY STEAKS**
Deluxe Dinners
Business Men's Luncheon
Children's Menu
Wedding Breakfasts and Receptions
Michelob on Tap
Fresh Seafood and Fish

Dancing
Nightly

**6600 Watson Road (9) — in St. Louis Hills — FL 6600-01**
Joe Mittino

walls. It later changed its name to Sunny Italy, owned and operated by Roy Russo. After a few years, Joe and Lo Parente, who originally owned a restaurant in the basement of the Melrose Building on Sarah Street, bought the building and changed the restaurant's name to Parentes Italian Village. Finally, it changed hands to the Garavelli's owners. Garavelli's still continues to serve some of the finest food in St. Louis, with home-style favorites such as pork chops and vegetables, delicious fried fish, and meatloaf with side dishes. The fried fish is particularly popular during Lent, when Fridays are no-meat days and Catholics in the neighborhood flock to Garavelli's for this delicious meal.

The comfort food served at Garavelli's is especially popular with the older generation. Another noted restaurant well-loved by the senior citizen set was Miss Sherri's Cafeteria, at the corner of Lansdowne and Chippewa until 2001. The St. Louis Bread Company now occupies that spot.

Garavelli's in 2008

Before it was Garavelli's, the restaurant was owned by the Parente family and became a popular eatery.

# Good Eats in the Neighborhood

I mo's Pizza near Hampton and Eichelberger opened in the 1960s. It was one of the first Imo's to open in the city and the last Imo's to make their famous pizzas in a brick oven. The Imo family lives in St. Louis Hills Estates. Steak and Shake stood at the corner of Lansdowne and Chippewa for many years, but it burned to the ground from a kitchen fire in 2001. White Castle at Chippewa and Hampton was a very popular restaurant that kept the neighborhood happy for many years. When the company decided to demolish the White Castle building in the 1970s, many neighborhood residents were up in arms. The daily coffee spot and hamburger destination was as much a part of the neighborhood as Hampton Village itself. The neighbors petitioned the company to keep the restaurant open, but the company declined and White Castle was torn down.

The Sand Trap and the Ranch House were notable restaurants and well-used meeting spots. Although it was outside the neighborhood, being located on Gravois Road just east of Christy Avenue, Lemmon's, owned by Curtis and Emma Lemmons, was a very popular restaurant with the St. Louis Hills clientele, serving some of the finest fried chicken in the city. Mom's Deli, near Lansdowne and Jamieson, is a popular lunch spot that often has lines of customers spilling out the door.

House of Pies stood at 4620 Hampton Avenue and opened in the early 1970s.

# Get Your Kicks on Route 66

Ⅰn the very early years of the neighborhood, a restaurant known as the Hampton-View Barbecue was a popular attraction. Featuring a well-known soda fountain and ice-cold watermelon, it had a perfect spot for business on the legendary Route 66; an estimated 22,000 cars passed by the restaurant daily. It changed hands, and in the late 1940s, it became the new location for a popular premier drive-in restaurant called Hoppe's, which had moved from Hampton just north of Pernod Avenue. It had the reputation as having "the best hamburgers in town." Hoppe's kitchen was reported to have all of the modern equipment enabling the cooks to make 1,800 hamburgers an hour. The carhops wore flashy red and white uniforms. The average order at the time totaled about 67 cents! The restaurant and its motto, "Hop in to Hoppes," were a part of the neighborhood until the early 1960s.

Another restaurant of note was the Parkmoor, which was on Route 66 across from Ted Drewes. It was originally Fassels, owned and operated by the St. Louis Hills neighborhood family of the same name. Fassels was known as a root beer stand. Many of these stands were wonderfully close destinations for children in St. Louis Hills throughout the 1930s and 1940s. When Parkmoor came along, Fassels was upgraded to a small restaurant.

Ted Drewes, on Chippewa, is the treat of choice for many St. Louisans.

Musial and Biggies, located at the northeast side of Tamm and Chippewa, was a popular dining destination for the St. Louis Cardinals baseball team and many sports enthusiasts. The location, originally called "66," was taken over by Julius "Biggie" Garagnani and his St. Louis Hills neighbor, Stan "The Man" Musial. It later became the Flaming Pit.

## Sweet Treats

Of course, St. Louis Hills can hardly be mentioned without referring to ice cream and frozen custard! Ted Drewes Frozen Custard stand on Chippewa is well known throughout the city and county, and its far-reaching popularity has made it a St. Louis landmark. One could simply say, "I live near Ted Drewes," and people throughout the region will know how to get to the St. Louis Hills neighborhood.

Ted Drewes was first established in 1929 when Ted Drewes, Sr., opened his first ice cream store in the state of Florida, and the St. Louis Hills location was opened in 1941. The tasty, signature treats are called concretes, and they are made with frozen custard blended with any number of ingredients. A delicious temptation! Ted Drewes truly became popular when the frozen custard was advertised on Jack Carney's KMOX radio program in the early 1970s.

On a hot summer night, Ted Drewes is the frozen treat spot of choice for St. Louisans. Police are kept on hand to keep order of the crowds that routinely spill onto busy Chippewa Street. When the weather turns cold and thoughts turn to Christmas, Ted Drewes becomes a fantastic Christmas tree lot. The trees are a tradition in many households.

In the early days of the neighborhood, though, Velvet Freeze was the most popular ice cream attraction. In the 1940s, Velvet Freeze advertised "one scoop for 6 cents and 2 scoops for a dime." Originally located on Chippewa directly across from Hoffmeister Mortuary, it was a neighborhood favorite. The shop eventually moved to Hampton, near Itaska, then to the east side near Delor. It featured an indoor stainless steel counter with stools. It finally closed in the 1980s. Baskin Robbins stood at the corner across from Ted Drewes for many years, but the competition was too steep. There also have been many snow cone stands throughout the neighborhood.

Dairy Queen still serves the neighborhood and delights many customers with its tasty frozen concoctions and hot food menu at the corner of Hampton and Eichelberger.

For years, many have said that the Donut Drive-In, just across from St. Louis Hills at Chippewa and Watson Road, has the best donuts in town. The neon signs and streamlined typical 1950s architecture still recall the days of Route 66. John Harter of St. Louis Hills owned the original establishment. In 1981, Tom Charleville of Thomas Coffee Company fame took over the business. After which, the business changed hands to the four Schwarz brothers, who still run the shop today.

Another noted donut destination is the St. Louis Hills Donut Shop on Hampton Avenue, just south of Loughborough Avenue, owned by Larry and Teresa Magnan.

These few establishments are only a cross-section of the groceries, drug stores, restaurants, and "hang-outs" that have been part of life in St. Louis Hills over the decades. While it is not possible to list them all, they all played an important role in the history of St. Louis Hills.

Donut Drive-In.

Kids (and dogs) enjoy summer evenings and impromptu games of kick-the-can.

# FUN IN THE CITY

## Leisure Time in the Neighborhood

F amily! St. Louis Hills was built around that one particular word. Cyrus Crane Willmore developed the neighborhood to ensure that "living was right for families," according to his many advertisements. Children were such a big part of everyday life that most articles in the *News of St. Louis Hills* in the 1930s and 1940s revolved around birth announcements, school functions, children's events, and birthday parties. Children walked to school, the parks drew youngsters and their parents, and homes were built to accommodate families. St. Louis Hills' children grew up and returned to the neighborhood to raise their own families, a sure sign that the neighborhood would thrive for many years to come.

Kiddie Land is well-remembered as the children's spot for fun.

# Kid Paradise

When most old-timers remember their childhood in St. Louis Hills, pony rides are often at the top of the list. According to many longtime residents, the pony rides at the corner of Hampton and Devonshire topped them all. Officially, it was called Hampton Amusement Park, but the children of the neighborhood simply knew it as "Kiddie Land." Although there were more than one of these small amusement parks, Kiddie Land was the longest lasting and most popular. Each pony had his or her name on a sign worn around its neck, and children would line up to ride their favorite ponies. Some of the bigger ponies were reserved for the "braver" kids. Kids also enjoyed boats in a tank, a roller coaster, Ferris wheel, train, cars, and cars on a track that were propelled by cranking a handle, similar to tricycle pedals. A variety of snow cones, candy, and soda were also available, making the site a true kids paradise! By the early 1960s, the demand for new businesses and the high prices for land meant the end of the beloved Kiddie Land.

Trains, ponies, and cars at Kiddie Land.

The corners of Hampton and Chippewa were also well-known "kid fun" areas. One of the most important childhood memories of long-time residents is the Traveling Carnival that used to set up on Chippewa, where IHOP is now located. The carnival eventually moved to the Target site. These were usually empty dirt fields, but once a year, the field was turned into a magical kid wonderland. The children looked forward to the carnival each year. The carnivals would last a week, and the parents were reportedly agitated with the kids' constant requests for money. When the carnival wasn't in town, the field was well used as a baseball diamond. Across Hampton, where Walgreens now stands, an open field served as a great place to ride bikes. The make-shift dirt track hosted many informal bike races.

Back in the 1930s and 1940s, kids made their fun in open, undeveloped areas. Before the Estates were built, children would frequent the open areas just south of Eichelberger. According to long-ago residents, a lake in the area was a popular fishing spot for the children. The kids were known to make forts and tree houses, keeping themselves well-occupied throughout the summer. The parents' only concern was the sinkholes that were reportedly part of the area. One longtime resident remembers a man living in an old shack on this property. He never bothered the kids, and the kids never bothered him, but they loved to play as if he was going to get them. His shack was eventually torn down when the Estates were developed.

# Park Perks

St. Louis's parks have always played an important role in city living. In St. Louis Hills, Francis Park and Willmore Park have been wonderful venues for fun and recreation. Francis Park was established in 1906 when David R. Francis dedicated sixty acres of land to the city of St. Louis. The original St. Louis Hills sprung from around the park, and it remains the core of the neighborhood today. Two recreational wading pools were the park's main focus. Originally, part of the park was used as a football field, but Francis Park also served as a prime spot for tennis and handball games, with many informal groups forming over the years. The park created

Swimming pool near the handball courts in Francis Park

the perfect environment for band concerts, playground get-togethers, picnics, photo shoots, softball and soccer games, and much more. Over the years, many walkers and runners with dogs and strollers have crowded the 18,000 feet of concrete sidewalks that surround the park. Numerous neighborhood residents and visitors have enjoyed strolling the 1,400 feet of "chat walks" that meander through the inside of the park. The beautiful lily pond has been the backdrop for countless weddings, parties, and even memorial services. Francis Park was created as the perfect spot for fun and relaxation. In 1935, the final cost of creating the entire park totaled $190,917.43.

Many stories have been part of the park's history. According to longtime residents, a kite-flying contest was held in Francis Park every spring. Each summer, day camps were held in Francis Park near the swimming pools with plenty of arts and crafts activities planned to keep the children busy. A Penny Carnival, used as a day-camp

The playground at Francis Park provides fun for families.

top: Francis Park's playground in 2008, recently renovated with up-to-date safety features.

bottom: Francis Park's playground in 1978.

top and bottom: **Run for the Hills brings out hundreds of athletes and volunteers, 1999.**

top and bottom: **Volunteers for the park cleanup, 2000.**

fundraiser and usually held in the fall, attracted many young families to the park. The children of the neighborhood look forward to the Easter Egg Hunt, a more than seventy-year-old tradition. The Christmas Tree Lighting, a ten-year-old tradition, brings many long-ago residents, young and old alike, together in the park. This kick-off to the holiday season features horse and carriage rides, hot cocoa, and, of course, the beautifully lit Christmas tree near Nottingham Avenue.

The Francis Park Easter Egg Hunt has been a kid favorite for decades. At right is a collection of snapshots from Easter circa 1975.

A longtime tradition in the neighborhood involves elaborate light displays on houses and entire blocks. The 6500 block of Murdoch has produced a yearly light display that's worthy of sightseers. Between Thanksgiving and Christmas, the block is simply known as Candy Cane Lane. The St. Louis Hills holiday lighting contests began in 1935. In the 1950s, the *Globe-Democrat* published an article about the contest that listed the winners' names and addresses. It was considered an honor to win, just as it is today.

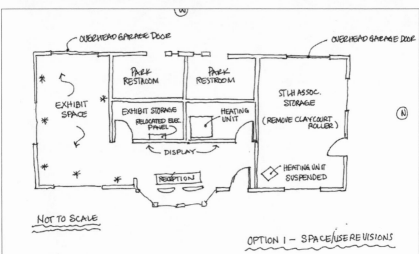

top: The maintenance shed near the playground was originally used as a caretaker's cottage.

bottom: A drawing of just one of the many hopeful plans that the neighborhood came up with for the cottage.

The St. Gabriel schoolyard draws a crowd during recess and after school. Courtesy Arteaga Photos.

Willmore Park became a part of the neighborhood in 1946 when Cyrus Crane Willmore donated seventy acres to the city for park use after he was appointed to the City Plan Commission. Combined with adjacent city-owned property, this land became Willmore Park in 1947. Willmore Park anchored St. Louis Hills Estates. The park is well known for its two ponds. On a warm summer day, kids and adults alike can be seen fishing from the banks of these lovely ponds. Geese and ducks are picturesque among the park's rolling, grassy hills, with its playground, roller skating rink, and paved paths adding to the park's appeal.

Perhaps one of the best-remembered aspects of Willmore Park were the stables that used to be housed at the southwest corner, very near Hampton and Gravois, called Valley Mount Stables. Beautiful riding trails meandered throughout the park, and children and adults loved to frequent the stables for riding lessons.

Longtime residents agree that the parks were the perfect spots on hot summer days. Without the benefit of air conditioning, the parks were open and breezy, creating havens of relief from the hot St. Louis summers.

Willmore Park offers stocked ponds for fishing, a playground, paved trails, and meadows.

# Pastime Good Times

B owling was an important part of the neighborhood in its inception. Stein Bowl, which was located at 3911 Hampton Avenue at the northwest corner of Hampton and Chippewa where the Lindell Bank building now stands, was a well-attended recreational spot. Many leagues were formed and games played. Stein Bowl boasted a snack and cocktail lounge that was a popular gathering place. Many women formed daytime bowling leagues. Stein Bowl was torn down in the 1980s, and the bank building was erected.

Red Bird Lanes, which served bowlers at the south end of St. Louis Hills at the northwest corner of the intersection of Gravois and Hampton, was owned by a consortium of one-time St. Louis Hills residents with famous names such as Musial, Garagnani, Berra, Schoendienst, and Garagiola.

Movie houses were also an important part of growing up in St. Louis Hills. Without television, many people enjoyed the movies weekly. The Roxy Theatre stood at the corner of Devonshire and Wherry for many years. Children would often walk to a Sunday afternoon matinee, spending a good part of their day and a quarter of their allowance to see a show. The kids would dig back into their pockets and purchase popcorn for a dime and a Coke for a nickel. Parents could send their children to the theatre without much worry.

The kids would generally sit in the front rows of the theatre, and the owner and ushers would patrol, making sure the kids kept quiet and well-behaved. The new movies came out on Tuesday evenings, so many parents and children would frequent the theatre on that particular night. Friday nights were popular with teenagers.

Other theatres regularly visited by residents of St. Louis Hills were the Kingsland at 6457 Gravois and the Crest at 8800 Gravois in Affton. The Crest was the first theatre to be built in greater St. Louis following World War II. In the original plan for the Hampton Village Shopping Center, there was to have been a large freestanding theatre about where the current Schnuck's store is located.

A Tuesday afternoon women's bowling league. 1937. Courtesy Missouri History Museum.

Children love to play in the front yards, finding friends and neighborhoods for playmates.

Fun and recreation in St. Louis Hills has changed over the years, but one idea remains the same. Families continue to be the focus of the neighborhood. Events are still planned with children in mind, houses are renovated to appeal to families, and the parks remain family oriented. Children continue to grow up, have families of their own, and return to St. Louis Hills.

Just look out the front door. You're sure to find a neighbor willing to play.

Monsignor Harry Stitz and Archbishop Joseph Ritter exit St. Gabriel's Rectory, then located at 4712 Tamm Avenue, to bless the cornerstone of St. Gabriel Church on Sunday, October 28, 1951.

# Chapter 4
# CHURCHES

S t. Louis Hills was built as a community with a strong religious foundation. In the late 1920s, Cyrus Crane Willmore planned the four parcels of land at the corners of Francis Park for churches, believing the religious roots would make the neighborhood stronger. Many families chose to live in St. Louis Hills, joining their neighborhood church and walking to services on Sundays. Longtime residents remember walking to and from church every Sunday morning. Socializing with neighbors and fellow parishioners was part of the Sunday tradition.

Each church was built with the neighborhood architecture in mind. Although the churches were built over a period of twenty-six years, the architecture is unique and in keeping with the times. The diverse congregations add another element of stability to St. Louis Hills.

# St. Gabriel the Archangel Catholic Church

St. Gabriel the Archangel Catholic Church officially began celebrating mass in November 1934 at the Cyrus Crane Willmore Real Estate offices. This served as the first parish church, with a congregation of about 150 families setting up for masses every Sunday. In June of 1935, the one-story school building, on Tamm Avenue near Nottingham Avenue, was completed and masses were held in the large basement auditorium.

The parish school opened in September of 1935. There were two classrooms, a chapel, and rooms for the first pastor, Fr. Skaer. In 1939, a second floor was added to the structure. The school was again enlarged by the addition of a new wing in 1946. Ground was broken for the present church at Nottingham and Tamm Avenues on March 5, 1950, and Archbishop Joseph Ritter dedicated the church on October 28, 1951.

The white stone contemporary edifice was designed by architects A. F. and Arthur Stauder. The traditional ecclesiastical design features have been retained, though the structure's plan is unique in that its trusses have replaced the usual columns in the nave. This provides for a fan-shaped seating arrangement with unobstructed visibility from all parts of the sanctuary.

The completed St. Gabriel the Archangel Church draws a large crowd to celebrate mass.

On Sunday, October 28, 1951, Monsignor Harry Stitz and Archbishop Joseph Ritter dedicated the corner-stone of St. Gabriel the Archangel Church in a public ceremony. Construction on the church lasted ten months.

A procession to St. Gabriel marks the first celebration of mass.

One of the first classes at St. Gabriel School. The elementary school children were grouped together in one classroom, while the older middle school children were in the other classroom.

In 1955, a new convent was completed at Tamm and Murdoch Avenues, with eighteen small bedrooms to house the nuns. In 1962, the new parish hall and gymnasium was erected. In 2001, a new addition and air conditioning was added to the school. St. Gabriel School has always had a well-known reputation for quality education and dedicated teachers and staff. The enrollment for the past twenty-five years has consistently hovered around 520 children. St. Gabriel's continued success can be attributed to the faithful families, many of them longtime residents, giving their time and talent to ensure the success of one of the city's most beloved institutions. The parish consists of more than 1,000 families.

top: St. Gabriel's convent dedication, 1955.

bottom: Monsignor Lubeley at a school picnic parade in the early 1980s.

top: The Class of 1987 marches in the school picnic parade.

bottom: St. Gabriel school picnic in the early 1980s. The picnic was held on the blacktop parking lot behind the church and school.

# St. Mark's Episcopal Church

S t. Mark's Episcopal Church, located at 4714 Clifton Avenue, has been part of the St. Louis Hills neighborhood since 1939. It was one of the few churches built in the Modernist architectural style in the world before World War II.

In 1871, Holy Innocents Episcopal Church of south St. Louis's Oak Hill neighborhood was founded. Oak Hill was basically a coal mining neighborhood. After many years and a declining Episcopalian population in the area, the remaining members of the church moved to more lucrative coal mining neighborhoods. At the time, development in St. Louis Hills was in full swing, and the Episcopalian St. Andrew's Mission was worshiping at Nottingham School as a temporary church. In 1938, Mrs. Anna Watkins passed away and left $75,000 to St. Andrews Mission. Bishop William Scarlett used this gift to build a church for St. Andrew's Mission, re-naming it St. Mark's. Bishop Scarlett was resolved to build a church on this limited budget, but he left the planning of the new church to the architectural partnership of Frederick Dunn and Charles Nagel. No church committees!

The dedication of the new church took place on January 15, 1939. Its architectural nuances were taken from the Modernist style of building. The church housed some unique decorations, such as the front of the choir loft, which uses neo-Egyptian detailing. In 1950, the tall, white brick church saw the addition of a Parish House and Rectory, all connected by a plaza, creating a beautiful white edifice among the neighborhood's lovely homes.

St. Mark's Modernist architecture is world-renowned.

St. Mark's grounds are serene and elegant.

The church's stained-glass windows are works of art. The north side windows depict the life of Christ based on the gospel of St. Mark. The south side windows explore Christ's presence in modern times—workers in overalls, strikers' umbrellas, soldiers, and moneybags are shown in the glass. Some of the south side windows also address the controversial issue of race relations—an important issue in 1939 as it is today.

The church's beauty extended to the Aeolian-Skinner organ in the choir loft at the west end of the church. It is an early example of a small, neo-Baroque church organ. In 1991, the All Saint's Memorial Garden on the north side of the church, which includes a marble fountain, was added. The garden's east side featured an old bell, dated 1636, that was shipped courtesy of the Royal Navy as a memento of a clergy exchange between the Village of Blendworth and St. Mark's from 1959–1960. The congregation today includes about eighty-five people, mostly from St. Louis Hills and the surrounding neighborhoods.

# Hope United Church of Christ

Hope United Church of Christ.

Hope United Church of Christ began on June 25, 1944, when sixty-three people met at the Nottingham School portable buildings and created a congregation in the neighborhood. The charter membership was held open until the end of 1944, by which time 154 people had united with the congregation. The land was purchased on the southeast corner of Francis Park, at the intersection of Tamm and Eichelberger Avenues, and ground was soon broken. The building was dedicated in 1950.

Growth was rapid. By 1952, plans were under way for a second building, which was dedicated in 1957. Over the years, Hope UCC invested much time and energy in outreach to the wider community. One beloved institution in the neighborhood, the HopeMark Preschool, has served families with young children since 1971. It is called HopeMark because it was founded initially as a joint venture of Hope UCC and St. Mark's Episcopal Church.

Hope UCC deeply commits its members to outreach partnership efforts like Habitat for Humanity, Lydia's House, Eden Seminary, and more. Over the past several years, Hope UCC renovated the main sanctuary to include a new pipe organ and more flexible furnishings. It also rejuvenated its small, historic chapel area and added a new playground and parking area to its campus. Lay leadership is strong, and the congregation continues to seek new avenues to serve Christ in this new era. The congregation's mission statement is: "It is the mission of Hope United Church of Christ, inspired by God's Holy Spirit, to engage people in living out the gospel of Jesus Christ."

HopeMark's Preschool Class of 2008.

top: **Cornerstone blessing of Ascension Lutheran Church.**

right: **Ascension Lutheran Church.**

# The Evangelical Lutheran Church of the Ascension, Missouri Synod

The Evangelical Lutheran Church of the Ascension, Missouri Synod, located across the street from the southwest corner of the park at Eichelberger and Donovan, was formed on November 20, 1936. That day, the decision was made to purchase a lot at the corner of Donovan and Eichelberger for $1,300. The main church structure was designed by Theodore Steinmeyer, architect, and George Moeller Construction Company was the general contractor.

In March of 1937, the officers were elected, and several months later a Charter Membership List was drawn up. The Reverend Erich Oelslaeger was installed as the first pastor in June of 1937, and the first baptism was performed in December of the same year. On June 2, 1940, ground was broken. The new church was completed with the dedication held on January 19, 1941. Ascension Lutheran, as it is informally called, continued to prosper. By the early 1950s, it became necessary to hold three services each Sunday as the congregation had grown considerably. It is also home to a Christian day school that currently enrolls about 330 students.

By the 1980s, the congregation had developed a plan for more growth. The plans included consolidating the church offices, meeting space, Sunday and Bible school classrooms, elevator service, equipment storage, a church library, and repairs to the school. In March of 1982, the rededication and dedication of the new wing was complete. The church also introduced a new hymnal called "Lutheran Worship." April 26, 2006, marked the seventieth anniversary for the congregation. Today, four services are held on Sunday for a congregation of more than 1,000 baptized members. While Ascension Lutheran is proud to be a part of the St. Louis Hills community, their membership is drawn from the surrounding St. Louis City and County neighborhoods. Its success can be attributed to it dedicated parishioners, clergy members, teachers, and staff.

A car accident at the corner of Eichelberger and Donovan with Ascension Church in the background, late 1930s. Courtesy Arteaga Photos.

# St. Thomas the Apostle Romanian Orthodox Church

St. Thomas the Apostle Romanian Orthodox Church was dedicated in 1959. It is located at 6501 Nottingham Avenue, near the intersections of Nottingham and Donovan Avenues. The cornerstone was laid on May 15, and the church was consecrated on October 12. This has long been known as a "family church" with members living in the same neighborhoods, visiting one another, and sharing their joys and sorrows.

Many of the founders are now gone, but their contributions remain and their children—the

St. Thomas the Apostle Church.

present leaders of the church—carry on. The parish council, ladies auxiliaries, and church school have all been influenced, shaped, and guided by this new generation of America Orthodox. The faithful of St. Thomas Church have preserved and continue to proclaim the Orthodox Christian faith. According to the St. Thomas Church, the future lies in the ability to remain an intimate and sharing community, to express love and unity, and to mobilize members' talents and energies for the proclamation of the Gospel of Jesus Christ in a world far different from the mountain villages of Albania, Macedonia, Greece, or Romania.

# St. Raphael the Archangel Catholic Church

St. Raphael, located in the St. Louis Hills Estates, was established in 1950, when Archbishop Joseph E. Ritter appointed Father Arthur G. Behrman to organize a new parish for the southwest corner of St. Louis City. In keeping with the tradition of nearby parishes, St. Gabriel and St. Michael (in Shrewsbury), St. Raphael was also named after one of the archangels. The church is built in the traditional colonial style, with four pillars flanking the front entrance. It was designed by A. F. and Arthur Stauder and reflected the style of the homes in the Estates.

The ground-breaking ceremony on January 21, 1951, was immediately followed by the excavation for the school. With encouragement of the parishioners, Father Behrman decided to build both floors of the school immediately, rather than build only the first floor and wait to add the second story. On September 12, 1951, the school was opened to 340 students. The children were taught by the School Sisters of Notre Dame. There was no convent, so parishioners volunteered to transport the nuns to and from the motherhouse on Ripa Avenue each day. On January 27, 1952, the first mass was held at St. Raphael. Although St. Raphael was built as a smaller parish than many in south St. Louis, the tight-knit community and dedicated parishioners ensure the success of this beloved Catholic parish.

top: St. Raphael's first First Communion class.

bottom: Procession from the old church to the new, 1966.

The interior of St. Raphael Church.

# St. Andrew Presbyterian Church

St. Andrew Presbyterian Church began in January 1949, under the guidance of the Reverend William Murdock and met in portable buildings at Busch School on Rhodes Avenue in the St. Louis Hills Estates neighborhood.

St. Andrew's first church building was located at 6933 Hampton Avenue, but when the lot on the corner of Loughborough and Southland became available, they seized the opportunity to purchase the land for $18,000. Ground was broken on December 20, 1959, with Harris Armstrong selected as the architect. The building's theme was taken from St. Andrew's vocation as a fisherman. The general style was built to mimic an upside-down fishing boat. The lights are suspended, depicting the fishing nets on a boat. The large stained glass window on the south side of the church has crosses at a 90-degree angle to signify the manner in which St. Andrew was crucified. St. Andrew did not feel he was worthy to be crucified in the manner of Christ and requested his cross be placed at an angle.

The new building was dedicated on January 17, 1960. The church is set back from Loughborough and Southland and includes a paved terrace to the south. The main floor is only three steps above grade and includes the church school and assembly room. The main floor contains a narthex at the south entrance, flanked on one side by a cry room and on the other by a small combination chapel, choir room, and bride's room. On New Year's Eve Day 2005, a fire severely damaged the sanctuary, yet the congregation banded together to rebuild the church.

St. Andrew Church is dedicated to mission projects, collecting food for area food pantries and clothing for families in need. The church has remained strong and dedicated to its south St. Louis roots. According to the St. Andrew's parishioners, the church's fortitude is shown by the resiliency and determination to not only rebuild itself, but also to be a significant factor within the community.

St. Andrew Presbyterian Church.